<u>Dedicated To:</u>
Natalie and Andrew Jordan
September 21, 2024

<u>Written By:</u> Abigail Gartland

I was born in Galilee in the first century.

When I was a young man, I believed in God but not in Jesus.

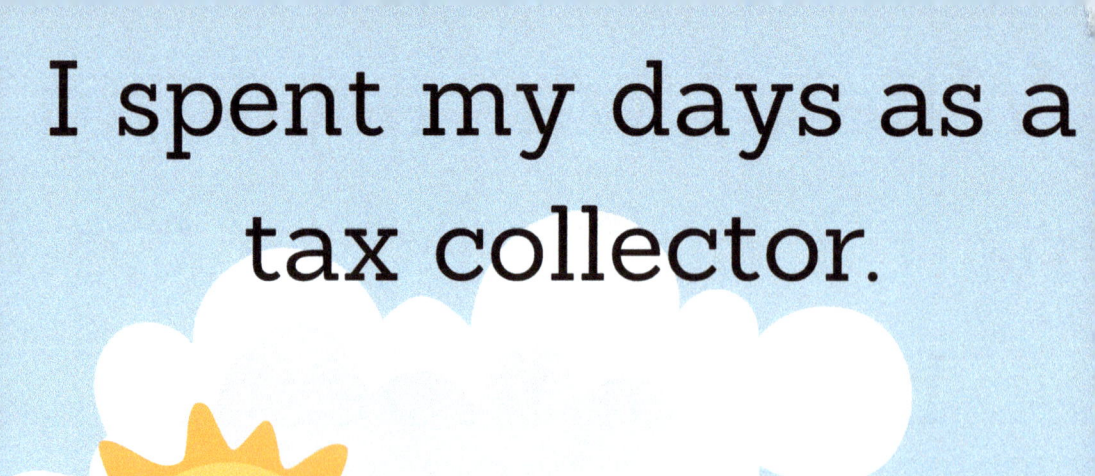

I spent my days as a tax collector.

That means I collected money from Jewish people to give to the Roman government.

This job let to dishonest behavior, and I was living a life of sin.

One day, I was collecting money when a man approached me.

He stood next to me and said "Follow me."

I realized this was Jesus, the son of God I started following Him. I didn't even think twice!

I followed Jesus and became on of His apostles to spread God's love and truth.

Throughout my life, I wrote down a lot of things that Jesus said and did.

I am one of the four gospel writers.

I spent the rest of my life spreading the love of Jesus with my brothers in Christ.

After a long life, I joined Jesus in the kingdom of Heaven.

Do you want to be more like me?

You can celebrate my feast day with me on September 21st.

I am the patron saint of bankers and writers!

I pray for you every day of your life.

St. Matthew, Pray for us!

Copyright:

Clipart: © PentoolPixie © LimeandKiwiDesigns
Licensed purchased: 1/10/2024

About the Author

Abigail Gartland

I love the saints and I love my faith. The idea for sharing the stories of the saints with little ones came when my dear friends were expecting their first baby. I wanted to create something as unique and special as our friendship. Each book is dedicated to very special people and groups who have enriched my faith in different ways. I am blessed to write these stories and appreciate the unending support of my family and friends. When I am not writing, I am a middle school teacher. I hope you enjoy these stories. I pray for each and every person who opens one of my books to learn more about the saints.

Abbie

www.ingramcontent.com/pod-product-compliance
Lightning Source LLC
LaVergne TN
LVHW051043070526
838201LV00067B/4902